365 MINI

Rebecca Dorothy Valastro

Copyright © 2011 Rebecca Dorothy Valastro

All rights reserved.

ISBN: 0-9954253-3-7

ISBN-13: 978-0-9954253-3-0

Published 2017.

All rights reserved. No part of this book may be reproduced by any mechanical, photographic, or electronic process, or in the form of a phonographic recording; nor may it be stored in a retrieval system, transmitted, or otherwise be copied for public or private use-other than for "fair use" as brief quotations embodied in articles and reviews-without prior written permission of the publisher.

The author of this book does not dispense medical advice or prescribe the use of any technique as a form of treatment for physical, emotional, or medical problems without the advice of a physician, either directly or indirectly. The intent of the author is only to offer information of a general nature to help you in your quest for emotional and spiritual well-being. In the event you use any of the information in this book for yourself, which is your constitutional right, the author and the publisher assume no responsibility for your actions.

I've taken the best of the best!

Within this book is 100 of my most favorite pages from 365: Positive Words for a Teenage Girl.

This travel sized, bag size, easy to carry, read, borrow and lend size, is easy to have by your side 365 days a year.

Be, see and feel amazing every single day, because YOU beautiful girl, are truly amazing!

- From my heart to yours -

B xoxo

I AM AS BRIGHT & BEAUTIFUL
AS A SINGLE FLOWER

WHAT I LIKE ABOUT ME

Write on a piece of paper 3 things that you like about yourself. It can be that you have nice hair, that you are good at sport or even that you have nice handwriting. Whatever you like about yourself, write it down.

Now every morning when you get up, read those 3 things to yourself and remind yourself of how great you really are.

I know it feels strange and seems kind of weird, but why not give it a go? When I feel sad and don't want to face the day, I read my list and I feel better. Sometimes it even makes me smile.

AND you don't have to stop there, you can write 10 things you like about yourself. You can write as many as you like. The best part is, on a good day when you already feel great, it makes you feel even better!

LIFE IS BRIGHT

AND SO AM I

I'M PRETTY FANTASTIC TOO!

BLAH BLAH BLAH BLAH BLAH BLAH

WORDS ARE ONLY WORDS UNTIL YOU PUT MEANING BEHIND THEM. For instance, Weird means Unique to me and is totally cool! Calling me a loser means you have poor judgment and you don't deserve my friendship. Sometimes, if someone calls me an idiot, instead I choose to hear, "you are soooooo intelligent!"

When people start using cruel words towards me, instead of feeling hurt I ask myself, how do I know exactly what they are thinking? Does it mean the same to me as it does to them? And if it's something quite full on like:

YOU ARE A FAT LOSER

Then I choose to drop a few letters of each word like a Y and an E and a T and an L. All of a sudden the words mean nothing at all:

OU AR A FA OSER

Makes no sense at all! The words are not complete because I don't allow them to be completed.

If someone calls you a nasty word or starts to pick on you, let a few letters drop, let the words drop. They really don't mean anything, because you are beautiful and perfect exactly as you are. You choose the meaning behind the words. If the words don't feel good, then I give them zero meaning at all.

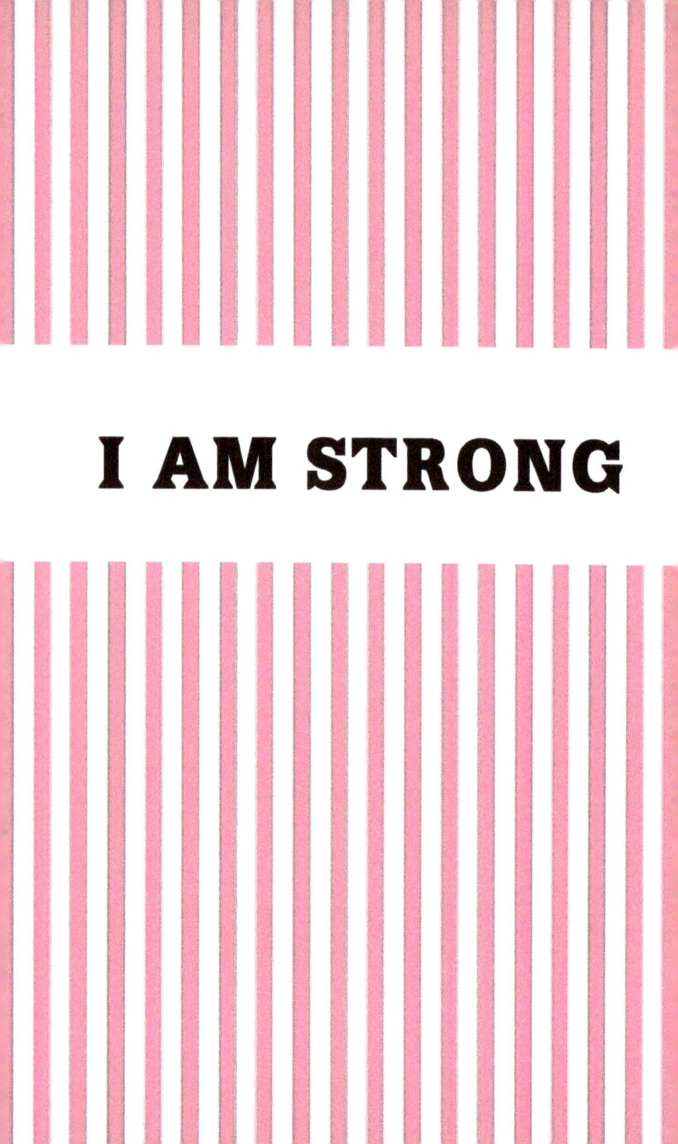
I AM STRONG

I know it feels weird when you start to say things like, "*I am pretty*" -especially when you are not used to saying them. How many times have you said to yourself, *I am pretty*? Let me tell you, YOU ARE BEAUTIFUL. Feels funny hearing that doesn't it! But it's true... and the more you say it to yourself, the less funny it will feel and the more you will believe it, because you are absolutely 100% BEAUTIFUL.

If You Can Dream it..
You Can Make
It Happen.

Dream Something
Awesome for Yourself!

With Planning Belief and Action
You Can Achieve Anything

All girls are special and gorgeous and deserve to be looked after. You deserve to always be treated kindly and loved. You are special and gorgeous too.

Sometimes when we are feeling bad, we lash out at other people. When we are hurting, we sometimes hurt others. It's OK, you are not alone. We all have done it. The best thing we can do, is recognize when we are hurting someone else and stop. All girls are special and deserve to be treated with kindness. Let your beautiful heart shine, sparkling from within, as you start the new craze; the kindness within.

YOUR EYES ARE BRIGHT
& BEAUTIFUL
YOUR EYES ARE BRIGHT
& BEAUTIFUL
YOUR EYES ARE BRIGHT
& BEAUTIFUL
YOUR EYES ARE BRIGHT
& BEAUTIFUL
YOUR EYES ARE BRIGHT
& BEAUTIFUL
YOUR EYES ARE BRIGHT
& BEAUTIFUL
YOUR EYES ARE BRIGHT
& BEAUTIFUL

I SEE THE BEAUTY
IN YOU
I SEE THE BEAUTY
IN YOU
I SEE THE BEAUTY
IN YOU
I SEE THE BEAUTY
IN YOU
I SEE THE BEAUTY
IN YOU
I SEE THE BEAUTY
IN YOU
I SEE THE BEAUTY
IN YOU

I hope you realize how special you are, how important you are, just as you are. If you ever feel like putting yourself down or you catch yourself saying something mean about yourself, I want you to HALT *it as soon as you realize you are doing it and replace it with...*

I AM A SPECIAL GIRL

YOU ARE A SPECIAL GIRL

Not everyone will like you and that is OK. I know it seems really important right now, but in 6 years time when you are working, in college or even travelling the world, this day won't seem so bad. Let the ones who are mean be the jerks, you have better things to do, like plan your future surrounded by wonderful people, living all your dreams till the very end.

THE
PERSON
YOU
SHOULD
TREAT
THE
BEST IS
YOU

There is no one else in
the world exactly like you.
That makes you pretty
Unique & Special too.

There is one YOU and
YOU have a very
important job to do
Being YOU.

YOU CAN REINVENT YOURSELF TODAY

Be whoever you want to Be.

With every rising sun, you
can choose to be different.

You can choose to be
anything you want!

If I saw you now, I would give you a hug. A hug is the best medicine anyone can buy. It makes you feel warm and safe inside, it allows you to wallow, scream and cry. And a hug does not necessarily have to come from another person. The most hugs I have had, has been from Teddy. Yep that's right my Teddy Bear. You are never too old nor too young, it's the perfect friend ready to hug. Teddy (my teddy bear) has certainly soaked up some tears. He was there for me when I thought no one else cared, he was there for me when I was too embarrassed and didn't want to share. He was there through the hurt and the pain, as my constant hug and confidant. Now a Teddy may not be for everyone, but hugs come in all sorts of shapes and sizes, like a mum or a sister and even your best friend. But if you ever need to talk to someone who doesn't talk back ... well then Teddy will always be your friend.

Is there someone you know who looks kind of sad? Could you ask them if they are OK? Sometimes the show that somebody cares, can make us all feel a little bit better inside.

IT'S OK TO FEEL BLUE

we all do sometimes

TODAY IS A NEW DAY

full of new possibilities

It's OK for me to feel angry and upset; it's normal. If the bad feelings don't go away, it's OK for me to talk to someone - no problem is too small to ask for help.

This moment will pass, as do all moments. One day you will wake up and you will be living the dreams you set for yourself. So make plans, take action and watch them come to life.

İ CHOOSE how İ want to SHİNE

I SPARKLE

No one shadows me

There is enough room for us
All to SHINE

Sometimes we need to be Willing to SEE it from another point of view. You never know what you might SEE.

There is no wrong way. It's about the choices you make. If you find yourself going in a direction that doesn't seem right to you, then make the choice to change directions.

I trust myself to know when to change directions, when to leave a bad friendship or bad relationship, when to study, when to work, when to play and when to take time out for myself.

Families come in all shapes and sizes. Some are blood related and some are your best friends. Family is those who support you, those who love you, those who will be there for you when you need them most.

GOOD FRIENDS ARE IMPORTANT

THEY WILL BE WITH YOU FOR LIFE. THEY WILL NEVER JUDGE YOU OR MAKE YOU FEEL BAD FOR BEING YOU. THEY WILL ALWAYS BE THERE TO SUPPORT YOU, EVEN THOUGH THEY MAY NOT AGREE, THEY WILL STILL LOVE YOU.

I Do MY Best
Every Day

I AM Really
Proud of ME

Look in the mirror & say to yourself

I am Loving & Giving
I am Truthful & Honest
I am Kind & Caring
I am Wonderful
I am Amazing
I am ME

It feels silly doesn't it... but it sure does feel good too!

It is OK to feel a little scared and uncertain about what tomorrow brings. Believe in your own strength and ability to get through it. You are more amazing than you think.

i AM STRONG
i AM SUPPORTED
i SUPPORT ME

WHAT DO YOU WANT?

Do you want to be able to run 3km? Shoot a basketball from the 3-point line? Perhaps you want to learn to dance? Talk in front of the class, audition for the school play or buy a new pair of jeans? Perhaps you want to be a Hollywood Star or even the next Prime Minister! Whatever it is begin by making a plan. A step-by-step process of how you will get there. You can make your dreams a reality. Through planning and action you can achieve whatever you want.

I have a vision board. A collage of people and places I like. It also has my dream career and the things I strive to achieve. I stuck this up on my wall and every morning when I wake, it inspires me and reminds me what I am striving for.

YOU CAN DO IT!
I KNOW YOU CAN
I BELIEVE IN YOU

Now go to the mirror and repeat:

I CAN DO IT!
I KNOW I CAN
I BELIEVE IN ME

What would you do, if you knew you couldn't fail? That whatever it was, you would be successful at it?

Think about it...

Have you got it in your mind?

OK... Now Do It!

What is it that's holding you back? If it doesn't work the first time, we can always give it another go. There are many ways to solve a problem as well as achieve our goals.

I RELEASE FEAR

I AM CONFIDENT IN ME

VIOLENCE IS NOT OK

It is not OK for anyone to hit, push or touch you. No one has the right to do so. If someone is hurting you, you have the right to say no and you have the right to tell someone about it, to ensure it does not happen again. Your body is sacred and special and it is yours and only yours. Say no to those who would act in violence against you and if you notice violence against someone else, tell someone you can trust, so it can stop. Violence is not OK.

Say NO to violence.

MY BODY İS SACRED. İ DECİDE WHO GOES NEAR ME.

It can be difficult not to compare ourselves to others - But you are your perfect You. There is no one else exactly like you in the whole entire world. I think that makes you pretty special.

Our bodies continuously change our whole entire lives. What you look like today will be different to next year. Everybody changes at a different rate, no two people change at the exact same time. Be kind to your body and nurture yourself, because you are worth it.

You are Bright, Beautiful and Wonderful. You can be anything you choose to be.

I create JOY in my world. People feel good when they are around me.

You know how this works now - so it's your turn! It's time to put pen to paper and write your own warm fuzzy. You can write one, two or even three if you like, the important thing is that you write at least one. Pick something you like about yourself and write it on a piece of paper and stick it somewhere where you will see it every day. That could be a spot next to your bed or on a mirror, in a diary or even in your wallet. Read this warm fuzzy to yourself every single day.

Now for something a little different but equally as important. Pick something you don't like about yourself and turn it into a positive. For instance, I don't like my hair and I don't like it when I get angry. So I wrote onto a piece of paper, "I have beautiful shinny healthy hair" and "I remain calm in every situation and I listen to what others have to say." Now it's your turn. You can write one, two or ten of them if you want to. Stick it somewhere where you will see it every day and watch how magically your thoughts can change.

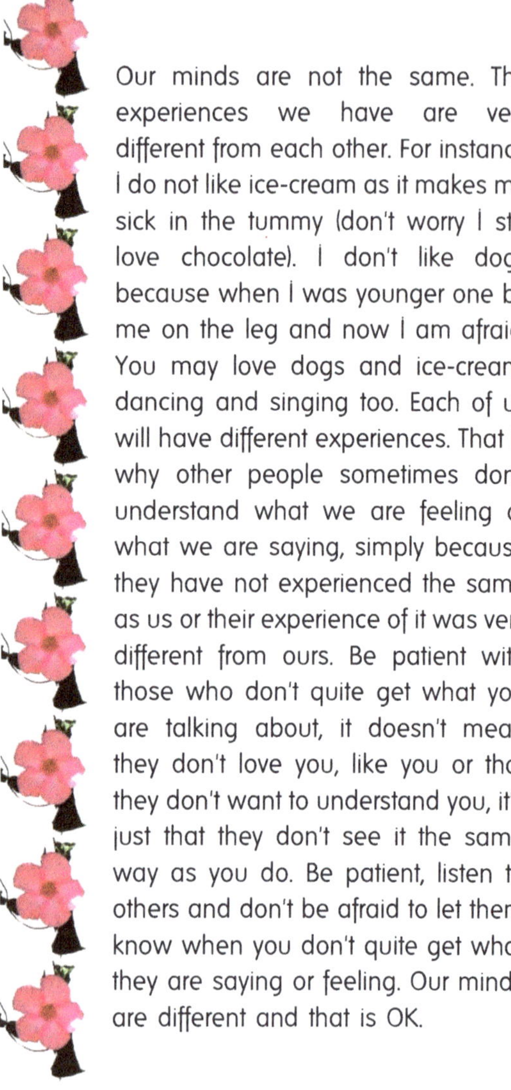

Our minds are not the same. The experiences we have are very different from each other. For instance I do not like ice-cream as it makes me sick in the tummy (don't worry I still love chocolate). I don't like dogs because when I was younger one bit me on the leg and now I am afraid. You may love dogs and ice-cream, dancing and singing too. Each of us will have different experiences. That is why other people sometimes don't understand what we are feeling or what we are saying, simply because they have not experienced the same as us or their experience of it was very different from ours. Be patient with those who don't quite get what you are talking about, it doesn't mean they don't love you, like you or that they don't want to understand you, it's just that they don't see it the same way as you do. Be patient, listen to others and don't be afraid to let them know when you don't quite get what they are saying or feeling. Our minds are different and that is OK.

My friend told me, it doesn't matter what other people think of you, it's none of your business anyway. I like this. I like this because we will never know what is in other people's heads, ever. We will never know what they are thinking or what they are saying when we are not around... and guess what, no one will ever really know what you are thinking about. We can tell people what we are thinking, but they don't really know whether we are thinking it or not. Thinking about what other people are thinking about us and thinking if they are thinking about what we are thinking, MY GOODNESS! EXHAUSTING! The only thought that matters is what you think of you. I know how hard it is to block out what you think people think of you, but you will never truly know. Focus on the nice things you have to say about yourself and the way you see yourself. Trust me, other people can see your inner beauty. Sometimes people are afraid of it and pick on you because of it, but it doesn't mean you're ugly. You are beautiful.

THE BEAUTY OF LIFE IS THERE'S SO MUCH TO DISCOVER...

SO MANY DIFFERENCES, SO MANY PEOPLE...

IT'S EXCITING TO DISCOVER NEW THINGS.

You may not get it today, but it is possible you will tomorrow and if not tomorrow, maybe the day after or the day after that. Persistence is the key. Try something new or a different way, but keep going. Most importantly keep believing, because I believe in you.

I WANT YOU TO HOLD YOUR
HEAD HIGH TODAY

BECAUSE YOU HAVE A BEAUTIFUL
FACE & A BEAUTIFUL SMILE
BEAUTIFUL HAIR WITH
AMAZING STYLE

WALK TALL AND PROUD
BECAUSE YOU ARE
AMAZING

Sometimes life can be confusing and feel pretty hard at times. When you feel this way come back to simplicity. Simply ask yourself, what is it that I want to achieve? Go back to basics. Is there another way this can be done? Stop and check in with your feelings, be honest with yourself. You are your greatest friend and you will always support yourself, no matter the outcome.

YOU CAN BE whatever you want to BE. Some people may say that it is impossible or that you're not good enough, but don't believe a word they say, YOU CAN DO IT. Choose what you want to be, then make a step-by-step plan and be willing to put in the work to get there AND above all BELIEVE, because YOU CAN BE whatever it is you want to be.

I CONTINUE TO GROW INTO

A MORE AMAZING PERSON
EVERY DAY

I CHOOSE TO SURROUND
MYSELF WITH

AMAZING PEOPLE WHO
SUPPORT ME

I AM UNDERSTANDING
I AM INTELLIGENT
I AM TALENTED
I AM CARING
I AM FUN
I AM AMAZING
I AM FABULOUS
I AM EXTRAORDINARY
I AM FANTASTIC
I AM BRILLIANT
I AM SUPER
I AM ME
I LIKE ME

The more you say it, the more you believe it. So if you don't believe it, I think you should say it at least 20 times today. You are all these things and MORE.

I AM
BEAUTIFUL

I WALK TALL AND PROUD

Squeeze your shoulder bones together in the center of your back. Tighten and tense your stomach muscles. Now walk and repeat:

I WALK TALL AND PROUD

If I feel nervous before walking into a room, I always use this trick. It always makes me feel better and more confident.

I'M WIDE AWAKE & ALERT

THE BUTTERFLY

So beautiful and free. Gliding through the air, peaceful and purposeful. Before the butterfly can become so free, it has to go through a transition. The start of its life begins as a little caterpillar, learning and growing, just as we are. We start off little and begin to grow, spreading our wings as we go. Our transition is not always easy and it can be quite tough, but have patience with yourself, because you are becoming that beautiful butterfly.

I AM BEAUTIFUL & FREE

I AM WHO I AM
I LIKE ME

GIVE THE MOST LOVE TO YOURSELF

when you feel good - others feel good too

BE YOUR
FAVOURITE YOU

FAVORITE THINGS… some of my favorite things are dancing, swimming, riding motorbikes, playing monopoly, watching soccer, SHOES!!! They can be high heels, boots, sneakers, flip flops… you name it, I like it! Our favorite things don't have to be the same, they can be girly and boyish or whatever you like. They are YOUR favorite things. Enjoy one of your favorite things today.

Sometimes it seems like everyone has it all together, that they aren't worried about anything, that they feel fabulous and great all the time and that they know exactly where they are going. Let me tell you, this is not the case. The truth is, we are all a little worried from time to time. We all think we are too fat, too thin, too short, too tall, too white, too brown, too loud, too quiet, not smart enough, not sure if I'll make it, break it, take it, you name it, we're all feeling a little unsure. No matter how old or young we are, we question. Even the most "together" people have their ups and downs, their days of doubt and giving up. The trick is to accept it when you feel that way and know that it shall pass. For you have endless possibilities and you are perfect just as you are.

I AM CAPABLE

I ACHIEVE ALL THAT

I WANT TO ACHIEVE

I KNOW WHO I AM

Write a description of who you are. Describe yourself in the most positive words you can think of. When you feel a little low, pull this description out and read how fabulous you are.

I KNOW WHERE I AM GOING

Write a description of everything you want to be, where you are going and what it looks like. Try reading this every morning and see how good it makes you feel. It will keep you focused too.

İ allow My CREATİVİTY to flow without inhibition nor QUESTİON. İ Pray that LOVİNG People Surround & SUPPORT Me and that İ ALWAYS have the Tools to follow through and COMPLETE the task with LOVE in My HEART.

i am capable of achieving anything & everything!

i hold the remote control to my life.

BELIEVE IN YOURSELF

BELIEVE IN YOUR ABILITIES

When a negative thought enters your mind and you begin to say, "I'm stupid, I'm silly" HALT IT and repeat to yourself;

I BELIEVE IN ME

If you can find a mirror, look at yourself and repeat it 3 times.

I BELIEVE IN ME
I BELIEVE IN ME
I BELIEVE IN ME

Find a mirror and sit in front of it. Look yourself in the eye and count to 30.

Can you see it? The sparkle? That special light inside your eyes?

Your eyes shine brightly, twinkling all of your possibilities.

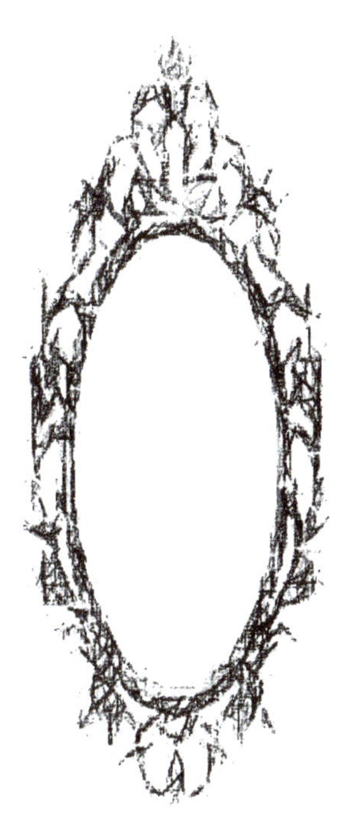

The Mirror is my friend...

I can see how Beautiful I AM

Close your eyes and imagine yourself at your very best. See yourself surrounded by amazing people and great friends. Does it make you smile? It makes me smile.

Feel AMAZING today
because YOU ARE AMAZING

Shoot for the stars...

No dream is too big when you take it one step at a time.

When I look up into the night sky and see thousands of stars, I know there is always hope. This moment, as all moments, will pass. There will always be new opportunities, new people, new places, in which I will go, meet and have. So look up into the night sky and make a wish, knowing that anything is possible for tomorrow.

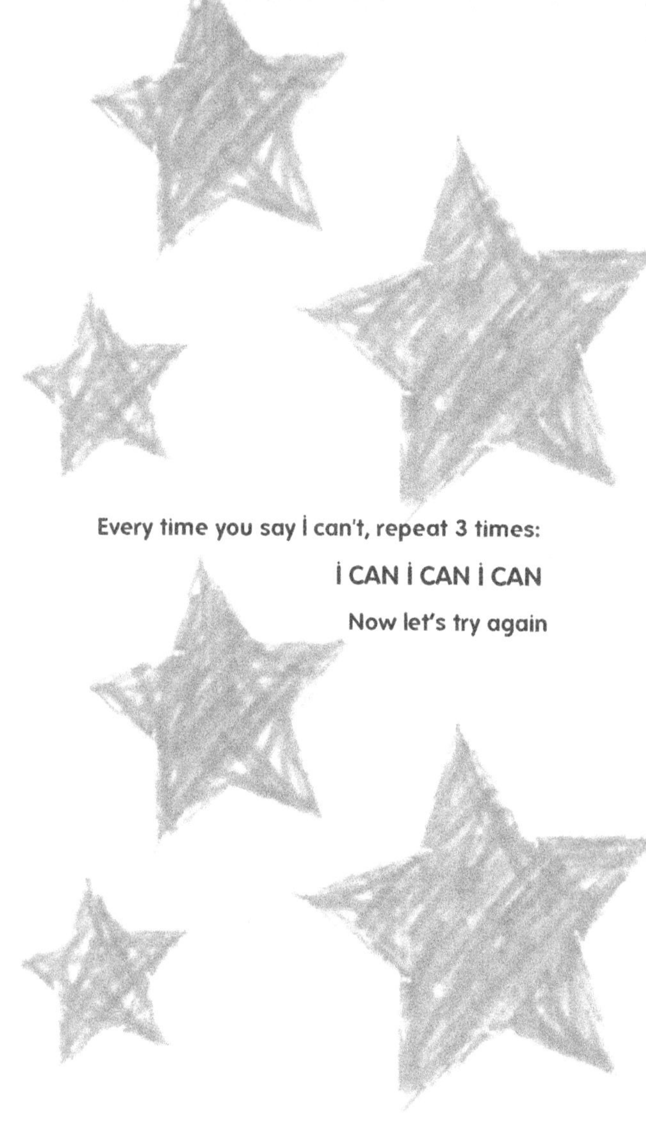

Every time you say İ can't, repeat 3 times:

İ CAN İ CAN İ CAN

Now let's try again

MAKE 3 WISHES

What are 3 things you can do

this week to help them come true?

No one else is in charge of your mind... so DREAM. DREAM BIG.

As far and wide as your imagination can cross, to the bottomless ocean and endless sky, there are no limitations, they are your Dreams.

DREAM FAR & WIDE.

I follow my

Dreams.

I can be, do and

have ALL that

I desire.

FRIENDSHIP

Is not about wanting to change someone to fit your life. It's about accepting them exactly as they are, being there when they need you most AND never saying, "I told you so." You must respect each other, listen to each other and say kind things to one another. A friend will never make you feel bad about who you are, just as you will never make her feel bad for who she is. Real friendship feels peaceful.

LOVE

Love, oh love! The stuff that makes you go crazy at times and act real silly too. It's OK, we ALL do it... but with true love, you never have to change. You are enough. You are You. True love does not stifle you, it does not stop you from growing, from living your dreams and being who you truly are. True love does not hurt you nor does it ever put you down. True love feels good.

The Dragonfly, much like the butterfly, represents change. This beautiful creature journeys through a deep transformation before taking flight. Like the Dragonfly, you will also undertake a huge transformation. You will emerge strong, graceful, beautiful. Stay true to who you are and nurture yourself along the way. YOUR best friend is YOU. Kind words must start with you. Your beauty is in a cocoon, building, ready to flourish. Share your beauty with those who nurture you, those who respect you, those who see you for the magnificent dragonfly within.

I HAVE THE
FREEDOM
TO BE
ME
& I LIKE IT!

I want you to take a colored pen and mark on the map where you are in the world. Make it a very small little dot. It's almost as though you cannot see the dot at all. I want you to imagine how many other little dots there are out there in the world. There are so many little dots, that it would be impossible to fit them all on this map. Sometimes it seems so important what the girl we sit next to in class thinks of us and the people in the playground, the ones we play sport against and the ones we hang out with at lunch, as well as the people we want to be liked by. It seems as though it matters exactly what each of these people thinks of us. If our clothes look OK, if we have the right hair, if we can play sport, sing the song in tune or even if we have painted our nails the right color. It seems as though it matters so much of what each person thinks of us that we forget what we think of ourselves. Not everyone is going to like the top we choose to wear, or what we had for lunch, how we walk or even how we talk. We aren't here to please every person. We are here to enjoy our lives. Not everyone in the world has the right pair of shoes or even a pair of shoes at all! So if today we get picked on or looked upon with disgust or spat at with cruel words, just remember they are only one of billions of little colored dots and what they say is so incredibly small against the whole entire world. There are many other people who have the same as me, less than me and more than me. It does not matter what they think of me nor what they say of me, because I matter to me.

This is so important that I think it's best we read this today and tomorrow, remembering that not only are we one tiny dot in the world, but so is everybody else.

I ♥ paris TO Smile

GO TO THE MIRROR AND SAY TO YOURSELF "I LOVE YOU"

AND SMILE - IT FEELS SILLY BUT THE MORE
YOU SAY IT THE MORE IT STARTS
TO FEEL REALLY GOOD!

TRY AND SAY IT EVERY DAY THIS WEEK

www.ingramcontent.com/pod-product-compliance
Ingram Content Group UK Ltd.
Pitfield, Milton Keynes, MK11 3LW, UK
UKHW062253290726
14090UKWH00017B/659

9 780995 425330